To:—
From:—

Illustrations Juliette Clarke
Written by Pam Brown

To my dear grandchildren
Emily, Thomas, Tabitha, Constance
                    Pam Brown

Other mini books in this series:
To a Very Special Daughter
To a Very Special Friend
To My Special Love
To a Very Special Mother
Happy Anniversary

Published in Great Britain in 1991 by Exley Publications Ltd
Published simultaneously in 1992 by Exley Publications Ltd
in Great Britain, and Exley Giftbooks in the USA.
Reprinted 1991
Third, fourth, fifth, sixth and seventh printings 1992
Eighth, ninth, tenth and eleventh printings 1993

Illustrations copyright © Exley Publications 1991
Selection copyright © Helen Exley 1991

ISBN 1-85015-265-9

EDITED BY HELEN EXLEY.

Designed by Pinpoint Design Company.
Printed and bound in Hungary.
Exley Publications Ltd, 16 Chalk Hill, Watford, Herts WD1 4BN,
United Kingdom.
Exley Giftbooks, 359 East Main Street, Suite 3D, Mt. Kisco,
NY 10549, USA

To a very special
GRANDMOTHER

Just remember, that a grandmother is the best
extra privilege any child ever has.

EXLEY
MT. KISCO, NEW YORK · WATFORD, UK

Grandmas are the best at keeping
secrets.

. . .

Grandmothers come to call carrying
shopping bags with Very
Interesting Bulges.

. . .

Grandmothers are about twenty
inside.
Sometimes six.

. . .

Grandmas don't just say "that's nice"
– they reel back and roll their eyes
and throw up their hands and smile.
You get your money's worth
out of grandmas.

WHAT IS A GRANDMOTHER?

Grandmothers are the people who take delight in
hearing babies breathing into the telephone.

. . .

Grandmothers are built to cuddle into, like a duvet.

. . .

Grandmothers eat anything you cook and say it is
delicious – even if it was a bit knobbly and sort of
horribly greasy. I think they have special stomachs.

. . .

Grandmas are good at sitting on the floor to play,
but they are terribly difficult to get upright again.

. . .

Grandmothers have bottomless handbags.

. . .

Grandmas bring flowers when your pet dies. And sit
and cry with you.

. . .

GRANDMOTHERS DEFINED

Grandmas sing crooked but nice.

. . .

Grandmas give you the cherry off the top.

. . .

Grandmas sometimes race you to the next lamppost
. . . but then they sit on a wall, and go a funny sort
of yellow.

. . .

A grandmother pretends you *can* give her a cup of
tea down the telephone.

. . .

Grandmas are really truly interested in
your dead frog.

Grandmothers have old feet and young hearts.

· · ·

All grandmothers like letters. Even if they just
consist of a squiggle and a dirty finger mark.

· · ·

My grandmother is good at climbing ladders. If you
let her take it slowly. And don't push.

· · ·

Grannies know what was there before you were.

· · ·

Grandmas outlast tyrants. That's why
the world survives.

· · ·

Everyone needs a grandma.

<u>A NEW BABY TO LOVE</u>

I thought I had forgotten how to hold a baby – but
my arms remember.

. . .

One day we think, at last, we have escaped the ties
of children, their troubles, their demands. And then
we feel a little tug – and find ourselves bound, once
more, by the needs of our grandchildren.

And their love.

. . .

No sooner have you stowed away the last teddy bear
in the attic than it has to be got down again.

. . .

How does it feel to be a grandmother?
A little odd?
It seems quite crazy that *your* baby should be sitting
there with a baby of her own on her lap.
But good.
A sort of bonus.

. . .

Those gasps of astonishment, those shrieks of
pleasure, those sighs of delight, lost long ago when
your children grew wise and worldly – are suddenly
given back to you by your grandchildren. What
seems to be the same small hands clutch yours,
dragging you from one excitement to another –
"Look! Oh look! Come *on!*"

. . .

Moms decide what is best for you when you are small. Grandmas decide what's most fun.

. . .

GRANDMOTHERS AND GRANDCHILDREN –
SPECIAL PALS

Grandmas and children take life a day at a time.

. . .

Grandmothers and grandchildren like stopping to look at butterflies and to talk to cats.

. . .

Grandmas and grandchildren going out for the day always look as though they are up to no good.

. . .

Daughters should always pretend not to see winks between grandmothers and children. It's better not to know what they've been up to.

. . .

Grannies whisk the extra green vegetables from your plate on to their own.

. . .

Grandmothers *agree* with mothers – but get them to change their minds just a little.

. . .

WHAT MAKES A GRANDMA GOOD?

Good grandmothers let you tell them the
entire plot of the film they too watched last
night on television. With suitable
amazement.

. . .

Ordinary grandmothers pretend to eat the
fluff-covered toffee you give them.
Good grandmothers *do* eat the fluff-covered
toffee you give them.

. . .

A good one doesn't mind if you crawl into
her bed at two in the morning.
Just as long as you don't wriggle.

. . .

Even the best of grandmothers is liable to
use totally unexpected language when you
play her a tune on your recorder at five
o'clock in the morning.

A good grandmother never kisses you unless
you want to.

. . .

Grandmothers must know stories. Book
stories and stories about your mother when
she was young. Stories about When I Was A
Girl. Stories one can't *quite* be sure are true.
Stories that are Absolutely True Cross My
Heart And Hope To Die. Grandmothers
must know rhymes. Grandmothers must
know the names of every plant, every tree,
every bird, every insect, every animal – and
oddities and wonders about each one of
them. Grandmothers must be able to draw
houses and dogs and cats and mothers and
fathers and YOU. And grandmothers must
be sensible and kind and just
and sympathetic.

Grandmas teach you fractions better than *anybody*.

They use blocks of chocolate. And they let you eat the sums when you're finished.

· · ·

Grandmas are sympathetic about the impossibility of doing some school work – and show you, very quietly and cunningly, that it isn't impossible at all.

THE BEST TEACHER OF ALL

Dearest Nanna, Thank you for teaching me knots
and knitting. Toffee making, bread making. Stars
and the care of cats. Thank you for introducing me
to Mozart, Scott Joplin and The Beatles, Van Gogh
and Renoir and Picasso, Charlie Chaplin and Cary
Grant. Thank you for the rules of tennis. How to
Polka. The bones of the body. Poker and cribbage.
The Morse Code. Semaphore. Why an aircraft
stays up. The habits of squirrels. The Beaufort scale.
How to give the kiss of life. Poppies and peonies
and the value of a good mulch. Martin Luther King.
How to get out of a skid. And the proper
way to curtsey.
It's all going to come in useful.
One day or another.

. . .

SURPRISED TO BE A "GRANDMOTHER"

Becoming a grandmother is wonderful. One moment you're just a mother. The next, you are all-wise and prehistoric.

. . .

Brace yourself. Before long she's going to be asking you about Life When You Were Young for a history project.

. . .

Clever, witty, capable, skilled. A very impressive lady. And best of all when you're sitting on the floor with your hair stuck full of feathers.

A lovely wife. A wonderful mother. And now a splendid grandmother.

. . .

When everything has sagged and you're feeling ready for the scrap yard, along come the grandchildren and hand you back your youth in a fancy box. Come on, grandma – get on your feet. You are starting all over again.

. . .

Grans never notice that they have become old until their grandchildren subject them to a detailed examination. Having carefully noted wrinkles, whiskers, brown blotches, silver hair, blue veins and drooping jowls, they comment, with great kindness: "You're *very* old, aren't you, Grandma?" When, of course, it's time at last to admit it.

. . .

FIT! MODERN! SO YOUNG!

You're everything grandmas in the old children's books were not. No mittens. No shawl. Scarcely a white hair. A taste for the outrageous. A yearning for adventure. Thank heavens.

. . .

Did no one tell you that now you're a grandma you're supposed to be *old?* Obviously *not.*

. . .

No one has as much fun as a grandmother on a toboggan.

. . .

Grandchildren think it amazing that grandmothers have such old skin and bones when they are obviously the same age as themselves inside.

. . .

Who is the one in our family who can out-walk, out-talk, out-cook, out-do, out-love everyone else? Grandma.

. . .

In you we have the New Improved De Luxe model grandmother. Same heart as the older types – but much better design, and just as cuddly.

. . .

It is remarkable how, overnight, a quiet mature lady can learn to sit cross legged on the floor and play a tin drum, quack like a duck, sing all the verses of The Twelve Days Of Christmas, make paper flowers, draw pigs and sew on the ears of severely-injured teddy bears.

. . .

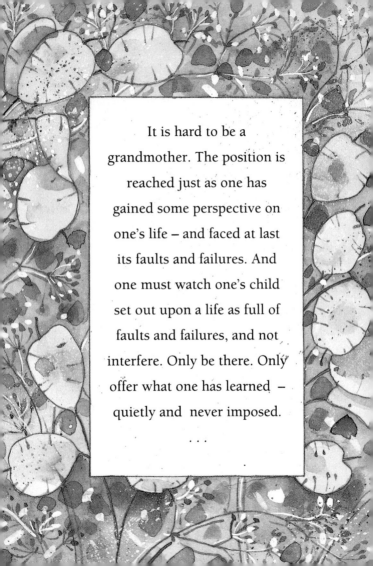

It is hard to be a grandmother. The position is reached just as one has gained some perspective on one's life – and faced at last its faults and failures. And one must watch one's child set out upon a life as full of faults and failures, and not interfere. Only be there. Only offer what one has learned – quietly and never imposed.

. . .

GRANDMOTHERS AND MOTHERS

I suppose a Victorian grandma stood and watched
her daughter coping with her first baby in her own
determined way and bit her tongue and hoped she
knew what she was about. And a Dark Ages
grandma. And a Plantagenet grandma. And a lady
dressed in smelly furs and a necklace of teeth.
Birds manage so well, doing it all exactly as all their
ancestors did, without any feathered grandmother
tutting at the approximation of an elbow. I suppose
it is part of the price of being human . . . give it forty
years and this red-faced scrap will be standing
in my shoes, watching *her* child with equal
respect and moderate alarm.

. . .

Parents are sometimes convinced that grandkids are
not just Difficult, but Impossible. It helps a lot to
have a little wise wrinkly to remind them just how
Difficult and Impossible *they* were.

. . .

THANK YOU, GRANDMA

Thank you for the time you were so sympathetic about my awful new school – even though you secretly remembered I felt the same about the last one. Thank you for being on my side when I told you all about that dreadful Sheila Parker . . . even though you'd never set eyes on her. Thank you for telling me that you hated pumpkin and spinach when you were my age. Thank you for helping me give the goldfish a proper funeral. Thank you for persuading my parents that I really *would* Come Out Of It.

. . .

Dearest Grandma. Thank you for showing me that I'm vital to the human race. Thank you for showing me that ancestors are people just like me - and that everyone in the whole world is related. Thank you for being my grandma and my best friend.

. . .

Thanks, grandma, for not wanting me to do the
sensible thing all the time.

. . .

Thanks for making *all* of us feel we are
of special value.

. . .

Grandmas listen when no one else will.

. . .

Grandmothers are in a position to say,
"Never mind, love. It will pass. *Truly*."

. . .

What makes a grandmother special is
that she is always there for us.
Always.

. . .

WISE AND KIND

Grandmothers come in dozens of shapes, bunches of wrinkles, languages, clothes, skins and stages of degeneration. But they all have exactly the same love in the middle.

. . .

Grandmothers are very good at picking up the pieces of something shattered beyond all mending – and mending it.

. . .

Grandmas are done with getting ahead and making a home and giving the kids a start in life. Grandmas have sorted out what is important and what is not. Grandmas give you a sense of proportion.

. . .

Dear Grandma, I wish I had your gentle smile and your kind hands.
I wish I had your strength.

. . .

I wish every frightened, lonely, sick, bewildered
child in the world had a grandmother to run to.

. . .

I love to hold your hands, Grandma.
They lead me back to the time before I began.
They keep me safe against the world outside.
They reassure me that I am worth a *lot*.

Grandmothers hold in their heads a world you never knew. Now they are giving it to you, to store with your own memories – to be handed on to *your* grandchildren in turn. Take it with care.

. . .

"Love and be loved," nannas say – "Learn to do a few things well enough to satisfy your heart, look about you, listen.
We are here so short a time."

. . .

You are the source of stories. You are the link with the past. You saw and heard and touched things that vanished before my mother and father and I ever came to be. You are from a world long lost - a world as familiar to you as this one is to me. You give me your life as a gift. I will keep it safe. I will give it to my children - and they to theirs.

. . .